The Blue-Green Housefly

Story by Janie Spaht Gill, Ph.D.
Illustrations by Bob Reese

DOMINIE PRESS
Pearson Learning Group

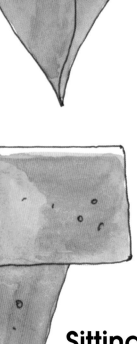

Sitting at the window
was a blue-green
housefly, laughing at
the funny world
as it quickly moved by.

2

3

First there was a dragon
riding a covered wagon.

Then there was a duck driving fast inside a truck.

Then there was a snake
rolling by on roller skates.

9

Then there was a goose
with a hat shaped like a moose.

11

Then there was a whale with a shovel and a pail.

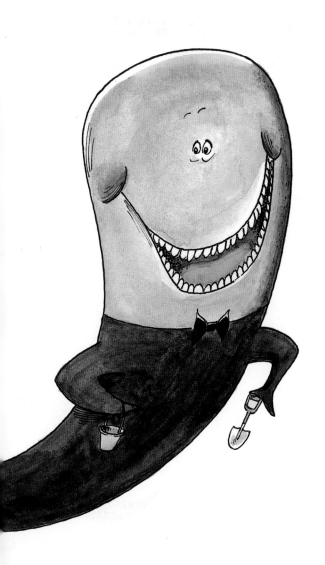

1

Then there was a cowboy frog riding on a dog.

Then there was a mule
doing a tap dance on a stool.

Then there was a rhino dancing with a dino.

It looked like so much fun,
he called out, "Wait for me!"

Not knowing what he'd
watched all day
were cartoons on TV.

Curriculum Extension Activities

- Invite the children to talk about the funniest part of the story. They could also draw a funny event not mentioned in the story. Have them write a sentence describing the event they've drawn while trying to rhyme the two nouns in the sentence. For example, "I saw an ape in a cape," "I saw a hat on a cat," or "I saw a star on a car."

- Use this opportunity to talk about compound words. Write the compound word housefly on a sentence strip. Then let the children observe you cutting the compound word apart to make two words: *house* and *fly*. Finally, mix up the two parts of several compound words and have the children sort them out, putting the two parts of the words back together.

- Have the children name some well-known characters from fairy tales. Write the names on the board and have the children cast votes for their favorite characters. Using the results, create a bar graph.

About the Author

Dr. Janie Spaht Gill brings twenty-five years of teaching experience to her books for young children. During her career thus far, she has taught at every grade level, from kindergarten through college. Gill has a Ph.D. in reading education, with a minor in creative writing. She is currently residing in Lafayette, Louisiana with her husband, Richard. Her fresh, humorous topics are inspired by the things her students say in the classroom. Gill was voted the 1999-2000 Louisiana Elementary Teacher of the Year for her outstanding work in primary education.

Softcover Edition ISBN 0-7685-2157-2
Library Bound Edition ISBN 0-7685-2465-2

Printed in Singapore
 2 3 4 5 6 7 8 9 10   10 09 08 07 06 05

Dominie
Press

Pearson Learning Group

1-800-321-3106
www.pearsonlearning.com